RUBANK EDUCATIONAL LIBRARY No. 88

RUBANK
INTERMEDIATE
Method

E♭ OR BB♭ BASS

J. E. SKORNICKA and E. G. BOLTZ

A FOLLOW UP COURSE FOR INDIVIDUAL
OR LIKE-INSTRUMENT CLASS INSTRUCTION

RUBANK®

HAL•LEONARD®
CORPORATION
7777 W. BLUEMOUND RD. P.O. BOX 13819 MILWAUKEE, WI 53213

FINGERING CHART
for
Eb and BBb Bass, Tuba and Sousaphone

Wherever fingerings are indicated, those below the note will apply to the BBb instruments and the fingerings above the note to the Eb instruments.

This method of indicating fingerings will apply throughout the book.

When only one set of fingering is used, it is an indication that such tones are out of the range of the Eb instruments.

NATURAL TONES

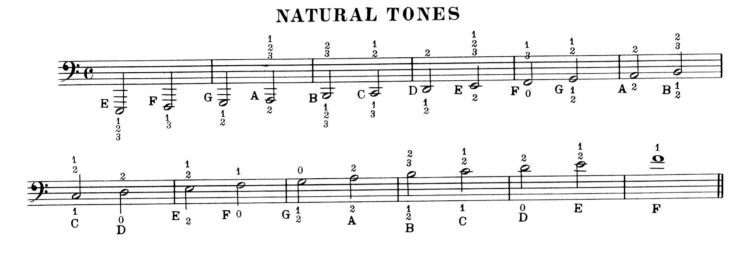

FLATS

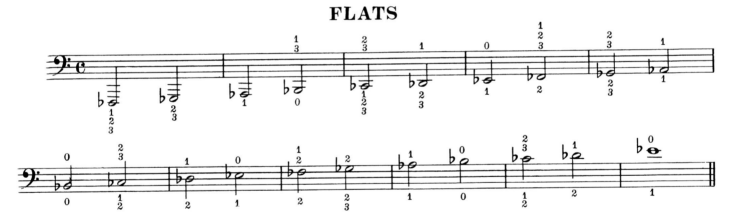

SHARPS

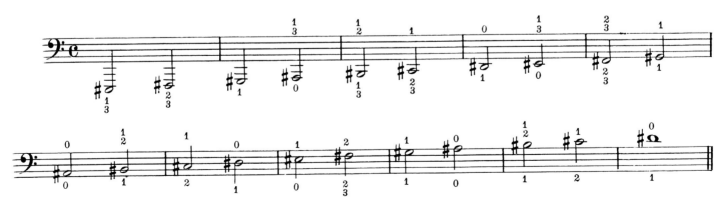

ESSENTIAL PRINCIPLES
of
Good Instrumental Performance

GOOD TONE is necessary in order that one's playing be pleasing to the listener as well as the player. Good tone can be produced only when the instrument is in good playing condition, equipped with the correct type of mouthpiece and played with the correct embouchure.

INTONATION: When two successive tones of different pitch are produced, it is necessary that each tone be in tune with the other, relative to the interval being played.

TUNE: The player must develop and train his ear so that a difference of pitch can be distinguished when playing with others.

NOTE VALUES: The player must develop a rhythmic sense so as to give proper value to tones as represented by the written notes.

BREATHING AND PHRASING: Each is usually dependent on the other. Since teachers of wind instruments differ on the methods of breathing, no special method is advocated, but it soon becomes evident to all players that in order to get good musical phrasing, it is necessary to breathe properly and in the proper places of a composition. It will be to the pupil's advantage to spend much time and effort on this phase of playing and take seriously all suggestions given by the teacher.

EXPRESSION MARKS: Expression marks in music are considered just as important as punctuation in prose and poetry. Good phrasing is the performance of music that has been properly punctuated. Expression marks put character into a mass of notes and if properly observed, will produce satisfying musical effects.

RELAXATION AND PROPER POSITION OF BODY AND HANDS: Whether playing in standing or sitting position, it is necessary that the body be erect and relaxed. Relaxation is the secret to the accomplishment of success in many other professions and trades. The arms must be relaxed, the elbows away from the body and the hands assuming a restful position on the instrument.

SUFFICIENT TIME FOR PRACTICE: Since different pupils require different types and lengths of practice periods, the objective that every pupil should establish is: "I will master the assigned task whether it takes ½ or 2 hours." The accomplishment of a task is far more important than the time that it consumes.

PROPER CARE OF THE INSTRUMENT: Carelessness in the handling of an instrument is the most prevalent handicap to the progress of young players. No pupil can expect to produce good results if the instrument is in poor playing condition. The instrument must be handled carefully and when a disorder is discovered, have it remedied immediately. Constant attention as to the condition of an instrument will pay dividends in the end.

MENTAL ATTITUDE OF TEACHER AND PUPIL: In order that the musical results be satisfactory, both the pupil and teacher must be interested in their task, and must have a perfect understanding of what that task is. The teacher must understand the learning capacities of the pupil so that the pupil in turn will get the type and amount of instruction that he will understand and be able to master.

J. E. S.

NOTE AND REST VALUES

1. The instrument should be in good mechanical condition, namely, slides loosened, and valves well lubricated. The condition of the instrument determines to a great extent the success or failure of the young player.

2. One of the important essentials in correct musical performance is a sound rhythmic conception. When this conception is established, correct playing will become an established habit.

3. Rhythms in succeeding lessons are fundamental, and their mastery will make playing fluent and comprehensive.

4. In playing the succeeding studies, special attention must be placed on the establishment of a correct embouchre. Although the general principle is the same, each individual player must discover the variation that will produce the best and easiest results.

Review Lesson

The care of the instrument is an important factor in the success or failure of a young player. Handle it with care and you will reduce the number of dents to a minimum. Dents contribute to faulty intonation as well as expensive repairs, to say nothing about the appearance in concert or on parade. Do not permit others to blow on your instrument, it is not only unsanitary but contributes to the size of a repair bill.

MARKS OF EXPRESSION AND THEIR USE

PIANISSIMO	*pp*	Very soft	FORTISSIMO	*ff*	Very loud
PIANO	*p*	Soft	FORTE	*f*	Loud
MEZZO PIANO	*mp*	Medium soft	MEZZO FORTE	*mf*	Medium loud
CRESCENDO	◁	Gradually louder	DECRESCENDO	▷	Gradually softer

In playing a crescendo or decrescendo the pitch of the tone should not change. ONLY THE VOLUME SHOULD CHANGE.

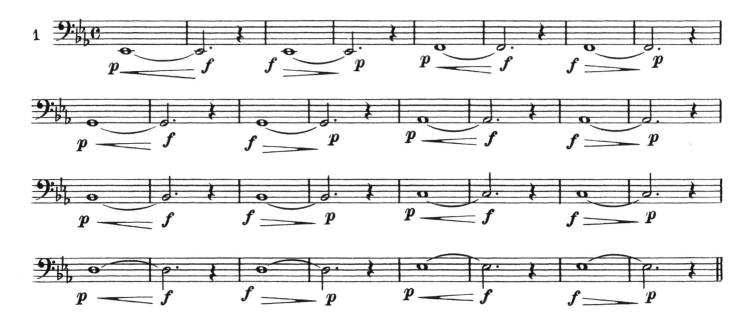

Play the following exercises daily at the beginning of each practice period. Think in terms of a big round tone and do not give up until that objective has been acheived.

The careful observance of expression marks is the usual indication that the player has been correctly taught and results in fine solo as well as band and orchestra playing.

All scales in succeeding lessons should be memorized. The good player always knows his scales and is usually selected for special assignments such as solo playing.

Expression Etudes

Slurs

STUDIES IN EXPRESSION

When playing either loud or soft, the quality of tone should not be affected. A common fault of the young player is playing sharp in **pp** passages and flat on **ff** passages. Special attention should be applied to this phase of playing.

Crescendo (cresc.) Gradually louder.   Decrescendo (decresc.) or Diminuendo (dim.) Gradually softer.

Neither pitch nor quality of tones should be affected in the playing of the sound graduations, namely, cresc., decresc., or dim.

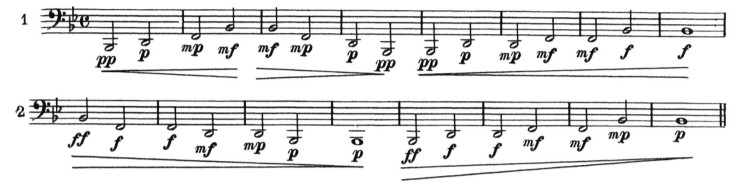

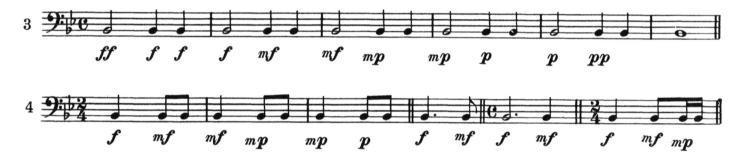

When a note is followed by a shorter note, the shorter one is played with less volume than the first. There are exceptions to this rule, however, players interested in solo playing will find this rule a great aid in properly interpreting music.

Using lines 3 and 4 as patterns, write in below each note the required volumes. This will acquaint the player with the sound graduations necessary in the playing of simple songs. When we hear players who play "with feeling" it is only a case of the player knowing and utilizing the proper volumes required by each note. This type of playing develops correct phrasing which in turn is the important phase of musicianship.

BLUE BELLS OF SCOTLAND

Moderato

Folk Song

A♭ Major Chord Studies

ETUDE ESPRESSIVO

A♭ Major Studies

Accents

The rinforzando (>) is placed over a note for the purpose of bringing out that particular tone more than the other tones in the same sequence. The accent (>) punctuates the important notes of a measure or phrase.

MARCH

ACCENT ETUDE

Dotted Quarter Notes

AULD LANG SYNE

Scotch

IN THE GLOAMING

ETUDE

F Major Studies

CHORD (F Major)

SCALE (F Major)

INTERVAL STUDY

MELODY IN F

D MINOR SCALES

Harmonic

Melodic

Staccato Studies

STACCATO ETUDE

STACCATO MELODY

MINUET

Interval Studies

F MAJOR STUDY IN THIRDS

E♭ MAJOR STUDY IN THIRDS

ETUDE

Syncopation Studies

¢ SYNCOPATION

2/4 SYNCOPATION

ETUDE

C Major Studies

CHORD

1

SCALE

2

INTERVAL ETUDE

Moderato

3

SWANEE RIVER

Andante

FOSTER

4

STACCATO ETUDE

Allegro

5

B♭ Major Studies

CHORD

SCALE

TONGUEING ETUDE

STUDY IN THIRDS

G MINOR SCALES

Harmonic

Melodic

Die Meistersinger

WAGNER

Moderato

RUSTIC WEDDING SYMPHONY

GOLDMARK

Moderato *molto*

simile

THE VOLGA BOATMAN

Russian Folk Song

Andante

Lip Slurs

When two successive notes of different pitch are slurred without the change of valves, it is called a Lip Slur. Lip slurs will appear in many succeeding lessons and are considered the most effective way of strengthening lip and face muscles. At first the muscles of the face will tire quickly but with daily practice will soon become strong and flexible. Flexibility of the lips should not be hindered by excessive pressure against the mouthpiece.

FLEXIBLE LIPS

Sixteenth Note Studies

HUNTERS CHORUS

B♭ MAJOR STUDY

Dotted Eighth Note Studies

MELODY

O TANNENBAUM

Folk Song

INTERVAL ETUDE

6/8 Rhythmic Studies

ETUDE IN 6/8 TIME

VIVE L'AMOUR

College Song

LIP SLUR MELODY

24

Triplet Studies

1

MELODY IN 6/8 RHYTHM

Moderato

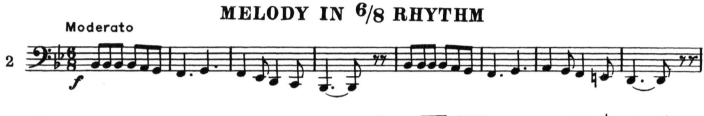

2

3

4

LONGING

J.E.S.

Andante

5

Chromatic Studies
ENHARMONIC CHART
(Same Tones)

CHROMATIC SCALE IN C

CHROMATIC SCALE IN B♭

CHROMATIC SCALE IN F

CHROMATIC MELODY IN B♭ MAJOR

CHROMATIC MELODY IN C MAJOR

CHROMATIC MELODY IN A♭

G Major Studies

Rhythmic Development

SAME MELODY IN 6/8 & 3/4

LEGATO MELODY

TECHNICAL ETUDE

Interval Etude

CHROMATIC ETUDE

RHYTHMIC ETUDE

D♭ Major Studies

CHORD

1

SCALE

2

TECHNICAL ETUDE

Moderato

3

SYNCOPATION ETUDE

Allegro

4

Chromatic Etude

LEGATO DUET

J.E.S.

Tongueing Studies

Huldigungsmarsch

GRIEG

WHEN YOU AND I WERE YOUNG, MAGGIE

BUTTERFIELD

O TANNENBAUM

German Folk Song

33

G Major Chromatic Etude

E MINOR WALTZ

E MINOR INTERVAL STUDY

E MINOR SCALES

Articulation Studies

G♭ Major Studies

CHORD

SCALE

CHROMATIC ETUDE

Moderato

E♭ MINOR SCALES

Harmonic   *Melodic*

G♭ Major Etude

GAVOTTE IN E♭ MINOR

37

Theme and Variations

VARIATION I

VARIATION II

Double Tongueing

For the playing of extremely rapid scale and chord passages, double tongueing is essential. Using the syllables tu and ku, practice the exercises in this lesson with care, VERY SLOWLY at first. After the tones produced with each syllable sound alike then begin to speed up the tongueing. A player on any brass instrument must practice this phase of playing diligently.

Theme

E.G.B.

VARIATION I

VARIATION II

VARIATION III

40

D Major Studies

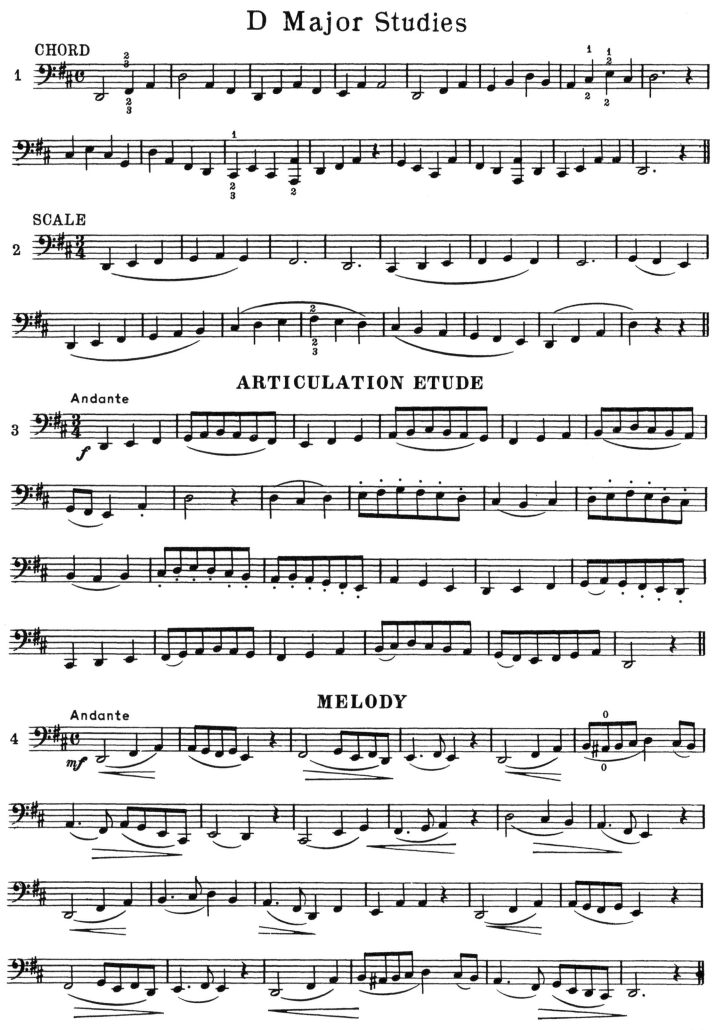

CHORD

SCALE

ARTICULATION ETUDE

MELODY

Abbreviations

EIGHTH NOTES

SIXTEENTH NOTES

THERE'S MUSIC IN THE AIR

ROOT

Moderato

POLKA

Allegro

Scale and Connecting Chord Etude

LEGATO ETUDE

GIGUE

Major Key Chord Patterns

Chords appear in Tonic — I, Subdominant — IV, and Dominant — V.

The tones that are the root of their respective chords are indicated by the addition of downward stems. The root of a chord indicates the step of the scale on which a chord is built.

I or Tonic means that "do" of the key is the root.

IV or Subdominant means that "fa" of the key is the root.

V or Dominant means that "sol" of the key is the root.

Frequent reference to and the practice of the chord patterns will develop a fluent technic and an intelligent musical conception.

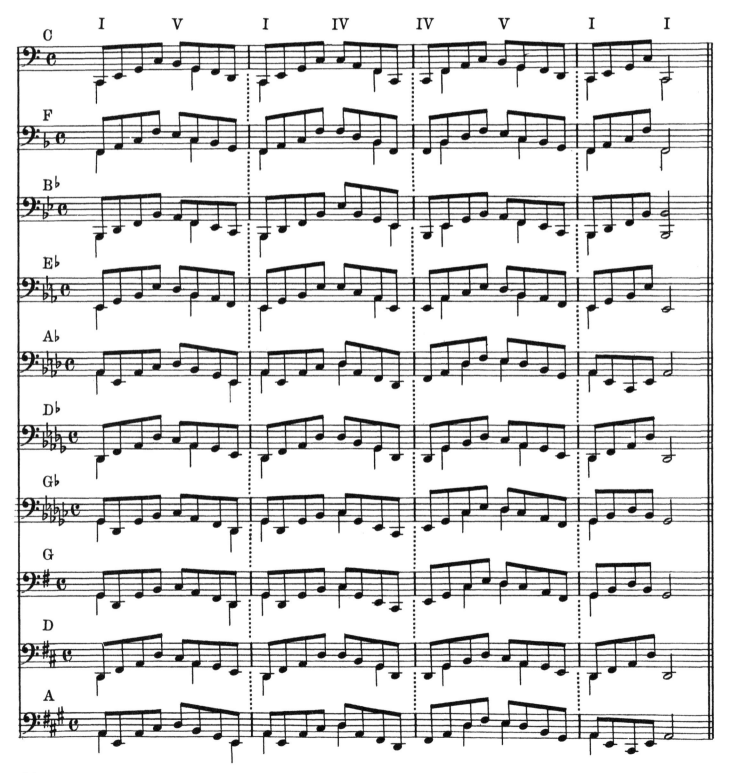

Minor Key Chord Patterns

The first step of the minor scale is <u>la</u> or the 6th step of the relative major scale. Therefore VI of the major key is called I minor to simplify the recognition of chord progressions. By the same token IV minor than is II major and V minor is III major.

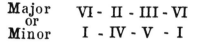

Major or Minor   VI - II - III - VI
                  I - IV - V - I

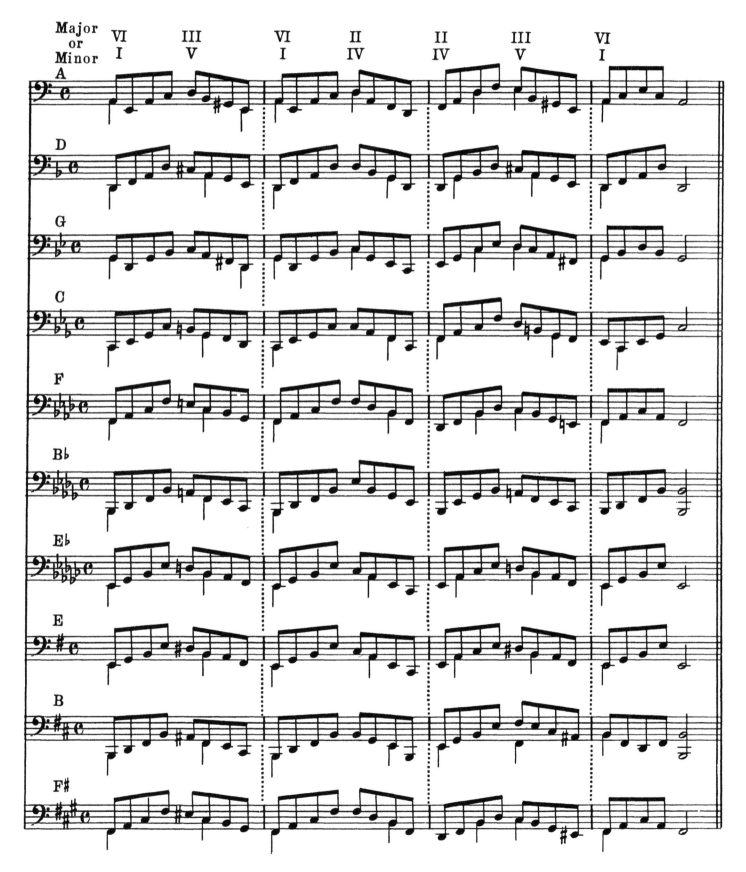

From
La Reine de Saba

GOUNOD

Moderato maestoso

From
OVERTURE 1812

TSCHAIKOWSKY

Moderato

Largo

Theme from
Les Preludes

LISZT

From
WILLIAM TELL

ROSSINI

From
WILLIAM TELL

ROSSINI

From
Oberon

Allegro con fuoco

C. M. von WEBER

From
SCHERZO OF 4th SYMPHONY

Allegro

TSCHAIKOWSKY